PIGS
and Peccaries

PIGS
and Peccaries

Annemarie Schmidt and Christian R. Schmidt

Gareth Stevens Publishing
MILWAUKEE

A N I M A L   F A M I L I E S

For a free color catalog describing Gareth Stevens's list of high-quality books, call 1-800-341-3569 (USA) or 1-800-461-9120 (Canada).

The series editor would like to extend special thanks to Jan W. Rafert, Curator of Primates and Small Mammals, Milwaukee County Zoo, Milwaukee, Wisconsin, for his kind and professional help with the information in this book.

Hippos are relatives of both pigs and peccaries.

Peccaries look similar to pigs but make up their own family.

Library of Congress Cataloging-in-Publication Data

Schmidt, Annemarie.
   [Schweine. English.]
     Pigs and peccaries / by Annemarie and Christian R. Schmidt ;
  [translated from the German by Jamie Daniel]. — North American ed.
      p. cm. — (Animal families)
     Includes bibliographical references (p.) and index.
     Summary: An introduction to members of the pig family, including the wild boar,
the Javan warty pig, and three kinds of peccaries.
     ISBN 0-8368-1003-1
     1. Suidae — Juvenile literature. 2. Swine — Juvenile literature.
  [1. Suidae. 2. Pigs. 3. Peccaries.] I. Schmidt, Christian R.
II. Title III. Series: Animal families (Milwaukee, Wis.)
  QL737.U58S3513   1993
  599.73 ' 4—dc20   93-13051

North American edition first published in 1994 by
Gareth Stevens Publishing
1555 North RiverCenter Drive, Suite 201
Milwaukee, Wisconsin 53212, USA

Series editor: Patricia Lantier-Sampon
Editor: Amy Bauman
Translated from the German by Jamie Daniel
Editorial assistants: Barbara Behm, Diane Laska, Andrea Schneider
Editorial consultant: Jan W. Rafert

Printed in Mexico

1 2 3 4 5 6 7 8 9 99 98 97 96 95 94

Picture Credits
A.G.E.—2, 7 (lower right), 11 (lower), 18 (lower); Emanuel Ammon—1; Othmar Baumli—9 (lower); Rolf Bender—13 (wild boar), 14, 16 (lower); Coleman—title page, 13 (collared peccary, giant forest hog), 16 (upper), 17 (upper), 24, 28, 30 (upper), 31 (left), 38; Comet-Photo—7 (lower left); Peter Dine—4-5, 13 (domestic pig); Hans. D. Dossenbach—4 (left); Faksimile-Verlag, Lucerrne—8 (from: Les Trés Riches Heures du Duc de Berry, 1984); Dr. Hans Frädrich—13 (bearded pig), 22; Werner Franke—12 (upper right and lower); Elvig Hansen/BIOFOTO—40; Jacana—Ferrero 4 (right): Jalain 12 (left): Maier 19 (lower): Mero 17 (lower): Schenker 11 (upper): Varin 13 (white-lipped peccary), 31 (right), 36 (right); Kinder- und Hausmärchen der Brüder Grimm, erste Gesamtausgabe von 1819—9 (upper); Max Meier—18 (left), 25; Sammlung Leo Mildenberg—6; NHPA—Bannister 13 (warthog), 26 (left): Blossom 13 (pygmy hog), 20: Krasemann 33: Lacz 39 (left): Leach 19 (upper): Pickford 30 (lower); William L. R. Oliver—13 (Celebes pig; Anon.: Pustels.), 23, 36 (left); Hannes Opitz—7 (upper right); Reinhard-Tierfoto—15; Dr, Christian R. Schmidt—13 (babirusa, bush pig, Chacoan peccary), 18 (upper right), 21, 26 (right), 27, 29, 32, 34, 35, 37, 39 (right); Swiss National Museum, Zurich—7 (upper left); Dr. Alex Stolba—10; Zoological Museum, University of Zurich—10 (from: exhibit catalog on "Pigs").

The Belgian Pietrain, a domestic pig, wears a coat marked with black or red spots.

Table of Contents

What Is a Pig?

Opposite, top: Weapons once used to hunt pigs included a spear called the "sow-feather" (very top). This spear had a wooden shaft and an iron tip that was 8-16 inches (20-40 cm) long. These three spears date from the sixteenth and seventeenth centuries.

Below: The pig as a toy. This Cyprian child's rattle, made of clay, dates from about 400 B.C.

The Pig in History

The pig can be found in the myths, folktales, and customs of many cultures. The pig was often a symbol for being well fed and rich. For some cultures, the animal was even the symbol of fertility and happiness. The Egyptians, Greeks, and Romans, for example, often slaughtered pigs as a way of thanking or honoring their gods. Many South Sea island peoples half-tamed wild pigs to later sacrifice to the gods. The ancient Germans revered pigs. The Germanic god Freyr rode a wild boar with golden bristles, while his sister Freya rode another golden boar called Hildisvin. But at the same time, the Germans also feared pigs. They believed, for example, that lightning in the sky was caused by cloud-boars tearing the heavens apart with their sharp tusks.

But, on the other hand, many of these same cultures considered the pig an unclean, gluttonous, and unreliable animal. For instance, a person who came into contact with a pig was expected to thoroughly clean himself or herself afterward. In these cultures, too, swineherds — people who tended pigs — were often looked down upon. In Ancient Egypt, for example, a swineherd could not marry outside of his group. This meant he could only marry the daughter of another swineherd. Because of the pig's terrible reputation, people of the Jewish and Moslem faiths are forbidden to eat pork. Even the Christian religion did not look kindly upon pigs because some people thought pigs were inhabited by evil demons. In the Bible's story of the prodigal son, the son's position as a swineherd is meant to indicate how low he had fallen before he finally returned to his father.

Good or bad, pigs and their relatives have been interacting with people for a very long time. As long ago as the early Stone Age, before any pigs had been domesticated, wild pigs were considered a particularly desirable catch. Drawings in the Altamira caves in northern Spain suggest that ancient hunters took great care in trying to catch aggressive wild pigs. The hunters painted images of pigs on the cave walls, probably as a way of immortalizing them.

As you can see, the image of the pig in society is a varied one. While you may already know the domestic pig of the barnyard,

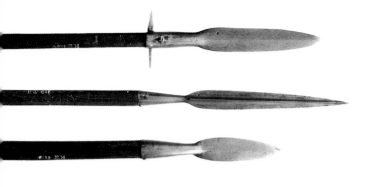

Below: Pigs have cloven, or split, hooves. This can be seen in their bones (left), feet (center), and hoofprints (right).

Bottom: The pig's snout with its sensitive disk is perfect for rooting in the ground.

Above: A Middle Ages hunting scene.

zoologists identify many families. So although pigs and peccaries are similar enough to belong to the same order, their many differences have led zoologists to classify each into its own family group. Pigs belong to a family known as Suidae. Peccaries belong to the Tayassuidae family.

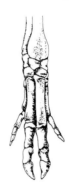

this book introduces an entire range of wild pigs with interesting behaviors and habits.

At Home in the Forests and on the Plains

Wild pigs make their homes in Europe, Asia, and Africa. Peccaries dominate the Americas, ranging from the south end of the United States to the heart of South America. Peccaries are smaller than most pigs, but they otherwise closely resemble them. Both pigs and peccaries — as well as hippopotamuses — belong to the same scientific order. This order, known as Artiodactyla, is made up of cloven-hoofed or even-toed mammals. The order also includes animals such as antelope, camels, cattle, deer, giraffes, goats, and sheep. Within the Artiodactyla order, however,

Both pigs and peccaries are highly adaptable. They live primarily in forests and bush lands, but they can also live on open plains and even in semidesert areas. Many of these animals live in the lowlands, while others prefer higher terrain where the nights

can be very cold. Depending on where they live, a species living in a cold climate will have a thick coat of hair, while a species living in a warmer climate is almost hairless. In Europe and northern Asia, wild pigs adapt to the changing seasons. During the summer, they look sleek and slim with short hair. In the winter, they are cumbersome because of their thick undercoats.

Omnivores with a Sense of Family

The African giant forest hog is the largest member of the pig family, weighing in at almost 660 pounds (300 kg), with a shoulder height of over 3 feet (1 m). Next to the forest hogs, adult pygmy hogs look like tiny piglets! In general, pigs have barrel-shaped bodies, short legs, and large heads. Wild pigs usually have long heads, while domestic pigs are more short-snouted. Some pigs have bumps and warts on their faces. Although these growths may look strange and rather ugly, they protect the animal's eyes when it gets into a fight or when it roots around in the ground for food.

At the end of the pig's snout is its snout disk. This disk, which is hairless and especially sensitive, functions as a "rooting shovel." This allows the pig to dig food out of the ground. The pig's canine teeth, or tusks, which continue to grow throughout the pig's lifetime, serve the same purpose. Hunters should beware of both the lower and upper tusks. The upper tusks don't grow downward, but rather arch upward. These dangerous weapons serve the pigs well in battle.

Pigs are omnivores. An omnivore is an animal that will eat both animal and vegetable substances. Pigs eat plants such as berries, roots, and mushrooms, but they will also eat insects, worms, frogs, fish, shrimp, mussels, eggs, young birds, small mammals, and carrion, or the remains of dead animals. In southern Asia, wild pigs have even learned how to crack open coconut shells.

With their small eyes, pigs do not see particularly well. To make up for this, they have an excellent sense of smell and an acute sense of hearing. These two senses can be more important than sight in the forest, especially since it is hard even for animals with good eyesight to see well through the thick underbrush. And as is often the case among animals with especially good hearing, pigs have developed a complex "language" that they use among themselves. A variety of grunts, squeaks, snorts, squeals, whimpers, and whines express everything from joy to fear to pain.

Pigs like to be physically close to others of their own kind. Sometimes they groom each others' coats and skin. This is a good way for pigs to show that they like and trust each other. But it is also useful since they are unable to do this for themselves because of their short necks. Pigs also groom themselves by taking baths in the mud, known as "wallows." Secretions are another form of contact among pigs. Pigs have many glands on their bodies that release a fluid substance

— called a secretion — with which they scent their environment, themselves, and other pigs. Despite having these types of glands, pigs don't have sweat glands. They can't perspire the way people can. To cool themselves off in hot weather, pigs must take regular wallowing baths in the mud. After a mud bath, the pigs will rub up against a tree trunk or stone in order to scrape off the coat of mud, along with the parasites and dirt that have gotten stuck in it.

A Nursing Order
Female pigs, called sows, usually bear large litters. In most species of wild pig, piglets are striped. Piglets of domestic pigs, on the other hand, are almost never striped. But both wild and domestic young pigs need a great deal of

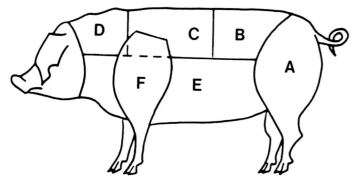

warmth in the days immediately following their birth. Because newborn pigs are unable to regulate their own body temperature, they will remain pressed up close to their mother and siblings for a certain length of time. This way, everyone warms everyone else, and family ties are established in the process.

The Pig in the Service of People

About nine thousand years ago, people who had previously led nomadic lives as hunters and gatherers began to settle in one place.

They began to raise crops and tend livestock. Among their livestock animals was the pig. Pigs were raised primarily to provide meat and fat. Only the Egyptians found another role for pigs. Egyptians drove great herds of pigs over their farmland in order to stomp old vegetation down into the soil. They were then able to plant a fresh crop. The Greeks and Romans enjoyed eating pork, which they smoked, dried, or made into sausage. They used the fat for cooking and frying, for lubricating the wheels of wagons, and for medicinal purposes. Even pigs' skin and the short, coarse hairs known as bristles were put to use. The strongest of these bristles grow out of the pigs' back and sides and are still used today for artists' brushes and hairbrushes.

Pigs are very intelligent and easy to train. They help people in many ways. For instance, pigs are used by police departments to sniff out hidden illegal drugs. In southern France

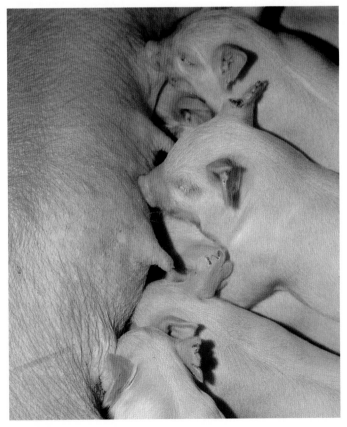

Below, left: The pig's fine sense of smell is put to good use in France and Italy where it is trained to root out truffles.

Below, right and bottom: The pig is also used to sniff out drugs and explosives. In Germany, a wild boar named Louise was famous for this. Trained by the police, she could sniff out such materials even when they were buried as deep as 29 inches (75 cm) below the ground.

and Italy, farmers take advantage of the pig's good sense of smell. There, domestic pigs are trained to sniff out truffles — a fungus that grows underground and is prized as a delicacy. Surprisingly, Vietnamese pot-bellied pigs are becoming increasingly popular as house pets, especially in the United States.

A Pig's Life

In the past, pigs were raised in pastures where they were able to roam freely with their families. They could enjoy taking mud baths, rubbing up against trees, or rooting in the earth. But today, unfortunately, most pigs live in dark mass breeding stalls. They must stand all day on chain fencing or lie chained up in solitary confinement. The piglets are taken too early from their mothers, quickly fattened, and slaughtered at six months. Alternative pig-raising methods would show the animal some compassion and respect. For instance, instead of mass breeding stalls, farmers could return to raising pigs in pastures, or use the so-called furnished family stall developed by Swiss zoologist Alex Stolba. Both methods would provide a pig with nearly everything it needs — places to hide, a clean place to eat, straw for rooting and building nests, and even a tree to scratch up against.

Pygmy Hog

Wild Boar

Bearded Pig

Bush Pig

A Guide to Pigs and Peccaries

Celebes Wild Pig

Giant Forest Hog

Javan Warty Pig

Warthog

Domestic Pig

Babirusa

Collared Peccary

White-Lipped Peccary

Chacoan Peccary

Wild Boars

Scientific name: Sus scrofa
*Length from head to rear: 35-78 inches
(90-200 cm)*
Height at shoulder: 22-43 inches (55-110 cm)
*Weight: Males 119-705 pounds (54-320 kg);
Females 97-271 pounds (44-123 kg)*

Wild boars are often referred to by hunters as black boars because of their thick, dark winter coats. Wild boars can be found over a geographical area wider than that of any of their relatives. Sixteen subspecies have developed from North Africa to Europe to Japan and Indonesia. Living over such a wide, diverse territory has led to differences in the boars themselves. For example, wild boars living in the north are quite large, while the subspecies known as the Southeast Asian pig are small and slender. In North America, Central America, and South America, the wild boar was introduced by Europeans as a game animal. Wild boars prefer to live in

Above: When grown, a male wild boar will usually live alone.

Opposite: With a mighty leap, a wild boar clears a stream.

Below: Young boars are nursed by their mother.

deciduous or mixed forests, where there is a plentiful supply of their favorite foods including acorns, beechnuts, and roots. In especially plentiful years, the boar will practically live on nuts alone during the fall. In general, however, the boar's diet also includes ferns, weeds, grasses, berries, insects, worms, lizards, birds, and even small mammals such as mice, young rabbits, and fawns. The boar will even feed on carrion or garbage. Much to the displeasure of farmers, wild boars also like to root in nearby fields for grain, corn, and potatoes.

In the forests, rooting by boars can actually be beneficial. The constant rooting keeps the forest floor porous, which makes it easier for new trees to take root. At the same time, boars keep the populations of mice and insects under control.

Wherever wild boars live undisturbed, they sleep at night and take long siestas at midday. In areas where they are heavily hunted, on

the other hand, the boars are active during the night and sleep all day in their hiding places. In general, wild boars live in family groups, called herds or sounders, in which there is a strictly enforced pecking order. The leader of the group is always an experienced sow, or female. The herd includes her grown daughters, several young pigs from last year's litter, and all of this year's piglets born by these females.

Grown male boars are loners who socialize with the herd only during the mating, or rutting, season when the sows are ready to mate. During this season, the powerful males will fight each other for the females. The males all line up opposite one another, circle around, and try to impress each other with their raised bristles. If this bluff doesn't frighten an opponent, the boars will resort to using their lower canine teeth, or tusks. These tusks, which are as dangerous as they look, can cause serious injuries. Fortunately, the males are protected by a layer of cartilaginous skin along their shoulders and flanks up to 2 inches (5 cm) thick.

After a gestation period of four months, the sow builds a litter basin of sticks and leaves. This is where the brightly striped babies come into the world. A female's first litter usually includes no more than five young. Older females may bear up to eight. If one female bears an especially large litter, other females in the herd will help her tend the young. They will even nurse the babies. When the babies are about two weeks old, both mother and young will return to the herd. Slowly, the little pigs' stripes disappear and are replaced with a reddish brown coat of fur. By the time they are about a year old, young wild boars look just like their parents. But many of the youngsters die from illnesses before they are a year old. In addition, the young are preyed upon by other animals or killed by hunters. Nature also works in its

own way to keep the number of wild boars appropriate for the food supply. In years when food is plentiful, many more young females mate and bear litters. In these years, older females will sometimes bear two litters. But in years when food is scarce, fewer young are born.

This Southeast Asian pig (above) is a subspecies of the wild boar (below).

Domestic Pigs

Weight: Mini-pig 88 pounds (40 kg),
Angler saddle hog 772 pounds (350 kg)

Domestic pigs evolved from the wild boar that makes its home in Europe and Asia. From bone remains, it has been discovered that the first domestic pigs were kept in Greece about nine thousand years ago. From there, they followed the spread of civilization throughout the world. The pig that lived about four thousand years ago in the region that is now Switzerland is a well-known specimen. It was a small pig that was apparently used by lake-dwelling people as a kind of garbage collector. It ate the garbage produced by people in settlements and, in turn, became fat enough to be eaten by people. Later, the lake-dwellers also kept two other types of pigs. One was a smaller, short-snouted pig, and the other was a much larger, long-legged pasture hog that was only half-domesticated.

Above: The Mangaliza , or "woolly," pig from Hungary is the only domestic pig that bears striped young.

The Greeks and Romans kept big meat hogs with floppy ears and short snouts. Often these animals were so fat they were hardly able to stand up. But by the fourth century, when Europeans began to migrate, this came to a stop. Then the pigs had to be able to travel. They had to be sleek enough to march along with the people.

Until the beginning of the twentieth century, different species of long-legged land pigs in Europe varied greatly in terms of size and color. At the start of the twentieth century, however, farmers in Europe also began to introduce English pig species, especially the Yorkshire swine. The Yorkshires were then crossbred with the local land pig.

Above: The Vietnamese pot-bellied pig is a favorite of children.

Above: The curly-haired Mangaliza pig is an older but sturdier species of pig.

Above: Weighing in at about 772 pounds (350 kg), the black-and-white Angler saddler hog from Germany is the largest domestic pig.

countries. Pigs are being bred today to produce more meat with less fat. In the process of trying to develop a better breed of pig, many older species of pig have died out. For example, there are only a few Angler saddle hogs left. These powerful black-and-white pasture hogs can weigh up to 772

Above: A litter of piglets in their straw nest.

The result was a floppy-eared pig, the so-called improved country hog. These pigs have become an important species of swine in Europe and America. Even today, there are almost no domestic pigs in Africa and Asia. And, since the Islamic and Jewish religions consider pigs unclean, strict followers of these faiths are not allowed to eat pork. Pigs are not raised, therefore, where these religions dominate.

Denmark is one of the leading pork-producing countries. There, a special domestic pig is being bred. The pig has four more ribs on each side of its body than normal pigs. This means the pig also yields more meat. Similar things are being done in other pounds (350 kg) and were once commonplace in northern Germany. Likewise, breeds such as the Hungarian Mangaliza hog and the woolly pasture hog could die out, since neither is very profitable any more. This last breed is particularly well suited for cold areas because of its thick woolly hair.

The pot-bellied pig from Vietnam is a domestic pig. It is descended from the wild boar subspecies called the Southeast Asian Pig.

Tame Wild and Wild Domestic Pigs

The process of turning wild animals into animals that will live and breed in tame conditions is called domestication. Breeders try to encourage characteristics in animals that will be the most profitable, such as the production of meat, milk, or wool. While this is an example of "tame wild animals," there is also such a term as "wild domestic animals." These are domestic animals that have re-adapted to the wild. Examples include dingoes, which were once domestic dogs in Australia, and mustangs, which were once

The mud baths that pigs regularly indulge in are important to their well being.

domestic horses in North America. The razorback in North America was once domesticated. This half-wild, thin, long-legged hog makes its home primarily in the southeastern part of the United States.

The improved domestic pig has erect ears.

Pygmy Hogs

Scientific name: Sus salvanius
Length from head to rear:
    Male 26-28 inches (66-71 cm)
    Female 21-24 inches (55-61 cm)
Height at shoulder:
    Male 9-12 inches (23-30 cm)
    Female 8-9 inches (20-22 cm)

Weight:
    Male 17-26 pounds (7.7-12 kg)
    Female 15-17 pounds (6.8-7.7 kg)

The smallest pig of all is the pygmy hog, which originally lived from the southern foot of the Himalaya Mountains in southern Asia to Assam in northeast India. Grown males of this breed can weigh 26 pounds (12 kg) at the most, and females weigh about half that.

Like their larger relatives, pygmy hogs root much of their food out of the ground, including roots, bulbs, worms, and insects. They also like to eat dirt, various plants, seeds, fruits, eggs, small animals, and carrion.

Unfortunately, these pigs are not only the smallest species of pig in the world, they are

Above: The pygmy hog is the rarest of the pig species.

also the rarest species. Today, the pygmy hog leads a threatened existence in its Indian homeland. There are several reasons for this unfortunate situation. For one, the little pigs have lost their habitats as people have taken over more and more land for agriculture and settlements. In addition, it is an old tradition in Assam to cover huts with a type of grass called elephant grass. But elephant grass thickets are also the favorite habitat and food of the pygmy hogs. Because humans use

great amounts of the elephant grass for their housing, pygmy hogs lose both their natural habitat and their primary food source. And without the physical protection of the grass, these animals easily fall victim to the daily threat of predators and poachers.

The International Union for the Conservation of Nature and Natural Resources has declared the pygmy hog one of the twelve most threatened animals in the world. India has taken measures to legally protect the little animal. In spite of these advancements, the numbers of the pygmy hog have been declining. In 1978, there were just one hundred pygmies left.

There are only three cases in which pygmy hogs have survived in zoos. A pygmy hog survived for a time in a London zoo in the nineteenth century. Another pygmy hog lived for a while in a Berlin zoo at the beginning of the twentieth century.

Finally, in 1976, a pair of pygmy hogs was brought to the zoo in Zurich, Switzerland. Here, an attempt was made to breed the rare animals. In the spring of 1977, "Cal" and "Cutta," as the hogs were called, became parents. The five tiny babies were grayish pink at first. They left the nest several times on their first day of life. The first brownish gold stripes appeared on the eleventh day, and it was also at this time that the young pigs began to have some solid foods in addition to their mother's milk.

Unfortunately, the male "Cutta" died when the young pigs were just three months old. The youngsters grew up nonetheless, following their mother around and around. The male siblings later had to be separated when they began fighting with each other. "Dira," the last of the females in the Zurich zoo, died in 1978 after a difficult labor. These were the last pygmy hogs to live in a zoo. Since India has forbidden the export of pygmy hogs, little can be done around the world to save them. Sadly, the animal may be facing extinction in the near future.

Above, left: Newborn pygmy hogs weigh only about 7 ounces (200 g).

Bearded Pigs

Scientific name: Sus barbatus
*Length from head to rear: 39-65 inches
(100-165 cm)*
Height at shoulder: 28-33 inches (72-84 cm)
Weight: 331 pounds (150 kg)

Bearded pigs have especially narrow bodies and longer heads than their relatives. This pig owes its name to a tuft of beard hair made up of long, white bristles that grows on its cheeks. The curly-bearded pig, a subspecies found on the island of Sumatra in Indonesia, has a beard that is tangled and curly even across the snout. The bearded pigs are all distinguished by four warts that mark their faces, two of which are usually hidden under their beards. They also are distinguished by double-rowed tail tufts, similar to the kind of tails that elephants have.

Above: This female bearded pig comes from the Philippine Islands.

Bearded pigs live in southeast Asia. They inhabit rain forests in the interior and mangrove forests along the coasts. With their narrow bodies, they are easily able to pass through even thick undergrowth. In many areas, however, the forests have been cleared or burned away by humans to such an extent that the bearded pig populations have dropped sharply.

For the better part of the year, bearded pigs, which live in family groups, stay in the same territory. They spend their days rooting the ground for roots and worms. With their long snouts, they are able to dig deeply into the soil. They also like to eat fruit and rubber tree saplings, as well as dead fish. Sometimes bearded pigs follow along behind monkeys such as gibbons and macaques, eating the fruit that falls to the ground as the monkeys swing through the trees. The pigs are also often found together with crowned wood partridges. These birds eat small seeds and insects dug up when the pigs root in the soil. The birds repay the pigs by picking ticks off them and warning them with loud cries when danger is near.

Researchers know very little about how the bearded pig raises its young. As is the case with wild boars, bearded pig females will split off from the herd when they are about to give birth. Then they build a hidden basin out of ferns, twigs, and palm leaves. Each litter usually has two or three young. The striped piglets remain with their mother for a year.

Bearded pigs also undertake long migrations. In herds of several hundred animals, they roam through the woods under the guidance of an old male. The animals always follow the same path at the same time of year. Unfortunately, bearded pigs make easy prey for other animals, especially when they swim through the water.

Opposite: At about four years of age, the male Celebes wild pig grows a shock of hair that falls over its face.

Celebes Wild Pigs

Scientific name: Sus celebensis
Length from head to rear: 32-57 inches
  (80-145 cm)
Height at shoulder: 28 inches (71 cm)

The Celebes wild pig lives on and is native to the Indonesian island of Sulawesi (formerly known as the island of Celebes). This warty pig lives in pairs or in family groups in high grass. It was brought to the neighboring islands of Timor, Flores, and Halmahera and eventually domesticated — but this occurred only near its home island. Apparently, the early inhabitants of Southeast Asia had the same idea as the human population in Europe when they domesticated the pig. They were mainly interested in preparing the animals as food.

On Papua in New Guinea, the Celebes wild pig was crossbred with the Southeast Asian pig, producing the Papua pig. Papua pigs live half-wild in the forests during the day but return to their owners at night. They are apparently able to distinguish between the drum signals of the various owners that call them home. This is just one more example of the intelligence of pigs.

Earlier, it was believed that the Celebes wild pig was a subspecies of the Javan warty pig. However, the Celebes pig is smaller and has shorter legs and a different head shape. Both animals, however, do have three pairs of warts on their faces. The warts help protect a pig's eyes when it is rooting and wallowing.

Before a female Celebes wild pig gives birth, she builds a basin for the litter. The newborn pigs are marked with five dark brown and six bright longitudinal stripes. When males are about four years old, they grow a comical shock of hair on their heads.

Javan Warty Pigs

Scientific name: Sus verrucosus
Length from head to rear:
    Male 56-75 inches (143-190 cm)
    Female 35-53 inches (89-134 cm)
Height at shoulder: 28-35 inches (71-89 cm)
Weight: Male 176-331 pounds (80-150 kg)
    Female 77-132 pounds (35-60 kg)

Female Javan warty pigs look tiny compared to the imposing males that are almost twice their size. The males mate with several females. Such "harems" also exist in other species, such as some monkeys, gorillas, and sea lions. In all of these cases, the male is a strong, heavy, and aggressive protector of the females. The size of the male is especially apparent when the animal is threatened. Then, the Javan warty pig raises its bristles, holds its tail high in the air in an "s" formation, and makes a shrill warning sound.

When a female Javan warty pig is about to give birth, she builds a big basin for the litter. She usually bears four to seven young. These young piglets have stripes that look more like rows of dots. These stripes are soon replaced by the yellowish brown coat worn by the parent animals.

In its Indonesian home territory, the Javan warty pig is often hunted or poisoned by humans. On the island of Java, its forest habitats are rapidly disappearing. And on the island of Madura, north of Java, this pig may have already become extinct. Certain zoos are making an effort to keep the species alive and more plentiful in the world. But many countries do not allow the import of pigs. Farmers are afraid that their livestock could be infected with diseases introduced by these animals. For this reason, it has been especially difficult to save threatened species of pigs like the Javan warty pigs, pygmy hogs, and babirusas.

Bush Pigs

Scientific name: Potamochoerus porcus
Length from head to rear: 39-59 inches
(99-150 cm)
Height at shoulder: 22-32 inches (55-81 cm)
Weight: 99-265 pounds (45-120 kg)

The bush pig is strictly an African species of pig. It lives in the forests and bush lands south of the Sahara Desert. It can also be found on the plains when tall grasses are growing there. Bush pigs are well adapted to their environment. With their wedge-shaped heads, they forge paths through thick undergrowth, all the while keeping track of each other by means of constant grunting and snorting.

Because this pig also likes to be in mud and the water where it can eat water plants, it is sometimes referred to as a "river pig." Bush pigs don't just stand in the water; they also like to swim and dive into it. They even swim to and settle on the islands of Zanzibar and Mafia off the African mainland and to the islands in Lake Victoria.

Bush pigs are found on both the African mainland and on the island of Madagascar. This is extremely unusual, since most of the animals that are found on Madagascar cannot be found on the African mainland and vice versa. This is because the island split away from the mainland thousands of years ago. Thus, the animals that were living on Madagascar island at that time evolved independently of their mainland cousins and are now quite different. But bush pigs came

Opposite: *A Javan warty pig wallows quietly in the mud.*

Above, right: *The colorful West African subspecies of bush pig is sometimes called the tufted pig because of the long tufts of hair that extend from its ears.*

to the island much later. Either they swam there themselves or they were taken there by people.

Among the thirteen subspecies of the bush pig, the tufted pigs are the most striking. They live in central and western Africa and owe their name to the tufts of hair that grow on their pointed ears. Their coats are among the most colorful and unusual in the animal world. Some have coats that run from red to dark brown and black; others are light brown or a combination of red and dark brown. The young look like their parents, although for the first few months of life, their coloring also includes light-colored stripes.

Bush pigs commonly live in groups of two or three, but sometimes their groups may have as many as eleven animals. Most groups seem to include only one adult boar, or male.

Groups of up to one hundred animals have occasionally been seen. Presumably the group has come together to eat foods such as ripe fruit. Both males and females also sometimes live as solitary animals.

Bush pigs spend all day looking for food. They root around for worms, bulbs, insect larvae, and roots. Often the pigs merely nibble on the roots, which allows the plant to survive. The bush pig diet also includes weeds, grasses, mushrooms, and favorites such as birds eggs, insects, snails, and frogs. Sometimes, like some of their pig relatives, bush pigs will follow along on the ground after chimpanzees that are swinging through

She will fearlessly fight even enemies that are much larger than she, slashing at them with her canine teeth. Her courage commands respect even from enemies such as the leopards. While the mother is fighting, the young pigs hide until she lets them know it is safe to come out.

Enemies are not the only ones who experience the more aggressive side of the bush pig. If certain members of the group — or just other bush pigs — get on each other's nerves, they will stand opposite each other and press their foreheads together. They butt heads and box each other with powerful snout thrusts, whipping their tails and

the trees. They gather the fruit that is knocked down from the trees.

The female bush pig gives birth to small litters of between one and four young. Like many other young pigs, the young bush pigs maintain a nursing order. Even if only one of the babies survives, as is often the case, it will continue to drink from the same nipple once an order has been established. It will maintain the rules of a large litter even if it doesn't have to compete with any siblings for food.

But whether she has one piglet or four, the mother pig will defend her offspring fiercely.

screeching in a way that indicates all should beware. Full confrontations are usually avoided through bluffing. In a bluff, the opponents show off their facial masks and powerful heads. After such a show of force, each pig then goes its own way.

Above, left: Because of the bush pig's wide territorial range, there are many subspecies. This pig comes from South Africa.

Above, right: Bush pigs also like to root in the dirt for food.

Giant Forest Hogs

Scientific name: Hylochoerus meinertzhageni
Length from head to rear:
    51-83 inches (130-210 cm)
Height at shoulder:
    30-43 inches (76-110 cm)
Weight: 220-606 pounds (100-275 kg)

The visitor to Africa who sees a giant forest hog for the first time often thinks at first glance that it is a hippopotamus or rhinoceros. The giant forest hog isn't quite that big, but it is far bigger than any other wild pig. It stretches about 6.5 feet (2 m) long and weighs as much as 606 pounds (275 kg). With its dark mane and powerful head, the old boar can make a very intimidating impression.

Despite their large size, it is easy for giant forest hogs to hide in their forest homes. For this reason, these animals were not discovered until 1904. Giant forest hogs live both in the forests and on the savannas of central Africa. With their thick coats, they can ward off even very cold weather conditions. In the Aberdare and Ruwenzori mountains, they live at elevations as high as 9,870 feet (3,000 m) and higher. The temperatures there at night can fall below freezing.

Giant forest hogs have only about thirty teeth, rather than the forty-four most other pig species have. On the other hand, their molars have more surface area than most other pigs. This makes it easier for them to chew grasses. Grass, in fact, is a major part of the giant forest hog's diet. In addition, these pigs eat eggs, fruit, insect larvae, and, occasionally, carrion. They are also especially fond of salt. The animals find this delicacy in termite-infested tree trunks.

Following a set daily plan, the giant forest hogs will visit their pastures, their salt licks, and their wallows. As they travel, the pigs move single file along paths through the woods. One or two strong boars will lead the group and are followed by the older sows, or females. Young boars and sows bring up the rear.   The young piglets travel next to their mothers or under their bellies. Along the way, each group will try not to interfere with other families that live in the same area. However, up to fifty animals from different families have been found together at particularly attractive sites or in open glades.

In the wallow, the pigs take mud baths one after the other. The pigs are sure to visit the wallow every day, especially in regions that are very warm. Here the animals find relief

Warts provide eye protection for the giant forest hog's face when it charges through underbrush.

from the heat and rid themselves of ticks and other parasites. After their baths, they rub off the crust of mud on tree trunks. Sometimes, they rub up against plants that release a sap. This sap coats the animal's bristles and eventually forms a sort of armor.

The boar is especially big and strong to protect his family. But pigs, in general, are

After a five-month gestation period, a female giant forest hog will give birth to from four to six young in a litter nest made of bamboo stalks. The babies are born straw-colored and have no stripes. Later, they will grow dark and look more like their parents. Fortunately, most of the young are born during the rainy season. This means there is

The African giant forest hog is larger than any of the other wild pigs.

quick to defend their group. If danger threatens or one of the group's members is wounded, other members of the family come to the rescue. When this happens, the younger animals are moved immediately to the middle of the group and surrounded by the adults. If needed, the boar will make use of his pointed tusks, which are up to 14 inches (36 cm) long. In fights with rivals, boars will grind their teeth and foam at the mouth. They rush at one another and crash their foreheads together. This can lead to fatal skull fractures.

plenty of fresh grass for them to eat once they are weaned and are no longer getting any mother's milk. The young pigs are entirely self-sufficient at the age of one and a half weeks. Unfortunately, it is not uncommon to find that only one piglet from a litter survives to adulthood. Many fall victim to the cold or to hyenas and leopards.

Warthogs

Scientific name: Phacochoerus aethiopicus
Length from head to rear: 41-60 inches
   (105-152 cm)
Height at shoulder: 26-33 inches (66-84 cm)
Weight: 106-315 pounds (48-143 kg)

hairless. On cold days, warthogs can be found pressed up close to one another for warmth. During hot weather, on the other hand, they rest in the shade to keep cool.

At night, warthogs return to abandoned burrows or holes in the earth that are cool during the day and warm during the night. The burrows, which are most often taken over

A warthog charges out of its den.

Like all of their relatives, warthogs are sociable animals. Usually, one or two females live together with their young and perhaps an older boar. Sometimes, several families will form a group. Generally, only females late in their pregnancy and older boars are found alone. But the warthog is different from most other species of pig in that it does not live in the woods. Instead, it lives on the open steppes of Africa. The warthog also differs from other pigs in that it does not have a thick warm coat. Its wrinkled gray skin is almost

from aardvarks, offer the hogs protection from their enemies. Many a lion or cheetah has stood in frustration at the entrance to such a burrow after its prey, the warthog, has suddenly disappeared into it. Usually, the young hogs are the first to head into the burrow, followed by the females. The males are the last down the hole, and they back into it. In this way, they are able to keep their eyes on the enemy as long as possible.

The warthog's head is large and angular, with intimidating tusks. The upper canines, which are about 24 inches (60 cm) long, are longer than those of any other pig. Often, the canines are uneven in length because one side is broken off in one way or another. This can happen during fights or when the pig moves rocks with its tusks.

The warthog has six warts on its face. The animal's eyes are set high and back in its head. This is important to the safety of the animal because warthogs are so long-legged they often must slide along on their wrist joints while eating grass. Their high-set eyes allow warthogs to keep an eye open for danger while they are in this eating position.

The warthog lives primarily on grass, and its jaws are well-adapted to this type of food.

Above: When warthogs hold their tails upright, they are signaling danger to other warthogs.

Although the animal has only a few molars, these teeth are long and flat and make excellent chewing tools.

A female will give birth to a maximum of four young at one time. These babies have thick, grayish-pink hair. After a week, the piglets leave the nest and begin to eat grass along with mother's milk. They spend their days playing games with each other. The skills the piglets learn through play are vital to them in their adult life.

Left: These male warthogs push each other back and forth with their heads in battle.

Babirusas

Scientific name: Babyrousa babyrussa
Length from head to rear: 33-43 inches
 (84-110 cm)
Height at shoulder: 26-32 inches (66-81 cm)
Weight: 95-220 pounds (43-100 kg)

The most striking member of the pig family is the babirusa. This animal also provides a special problem for zoologists because fossil findings indicate that it is more closely related to the hippopotamus family than to its own pig family.

Above and above, right: The tusks of the male babirusa look like the antlers of a male deer.

In the language of the native populations where the animal is found, *babi* means "pig" and *rusa* means "deer." How the animal came to get this name is obvious from its appearance. While it physically resembles a pig, the giant canines of the older babirusa boars are reminiscent of a deer's antlers. The upper canines, which are either very small or nonexistent on the females, grow through the upper snouts of males when they are about a year and a half old. With many other types of pigs, the upper canines meet the lower canines. In the case of the babirusa, however, the tusks curve back up toward the pig's face and sometimes grow back through the skin into the nose bones. These tusks are a sign of rank among the males, just as the male deer's antlers are for him.

In fights with rivals, the boar does not attack with its upper canines, which can easily break, but with its lower canines. Usually an open mouth and glowering eyes are enough to scare the rival. When they are not, the rivals butt into each other using their snouts. If this doesn't settle the matter, the rivals get up on their hind legs and tear into each other with their front hooves like boxers.

Babirusas are native to the islands of Indonesia, including the Moluccas, the island of Sulawesi, and the little island of Togian. The Celebes babirusa has only very short bristles and is almost hairless with a tiny tuft on its tail. It has the longest and strongest canine teeth of the subspecies. The babirusas on Togian have dark brownish black hair.

like to wallow, and they are good swimmers that sometimes swim to another island. They like to eat mangoes and other fruits, as well as fungi, nettles, insects, leaves, and also nuts, which they crack open themselves. People often hunt babirusa pigs for their meat. Their greatest threat, however, is the deforestation of their habitats.

Compared to the male, the female babirusa (above) has small canine teeth.

Only about one hundred of these animals remain. The Moluccan babirusa is smaller than the other two and has long, thick hair that is black, golden, or a mixture of the two.

Researchers on the little island of Pangempan have observed that babirusas remain active during the day as well as at night, whether individually or in small groups. They always use the same forest paths. They

Babirusas bear one, two, or occasionally three young after a gestation period of four to five months. To help the pig's populations, zoos across Europe have tried to increase their numbers through breeding programs. For babirusas raised in zoos to return to the wild, however, there would still need to be sufficient forested areas in which they could make their homes.

Peccaries

The name *peccary* comes from the language of the Brazilian Tupi Indians and means "an animal that takes many paths through the woods." This is precisely what peccaries do. These animals, also called javelinas or musk hogs, make their homes in the woods from Arizona all the way south to Argentina. The Indians of Central and South America have had a close relationship with the animals for years.

Three types of peccaries exist. All three resemble their relatives in the pig family with their big heads, snouts, and bristles. Like pigs, they are sociable animals that like to cuddle up next to one another.

But there are also many differences between pigs and peccaries. Unlike pigs, peccary babies are usually born in sets of twins. Peccaries have stomachs that look more like cow stomachs than pig stomachs, and the bones in their feet are fused together, unlike those of pigs. The peccary's tail is also shorter than that of most pigs. Further, peccaries have only thirty-eight teeth, while most pigs have forty-four. The upper canines of most of the pig species grow outward and upward, but the peccary's upper canine teeth grow downward. They grind together with the lower canines to form a sharp biting weapon. One of the peccary's most interesting differences is that it has a gland called a musk gland that secretes a foul-smelling substance when the animal is attacked. Between this musk gland and its teeth, the peccary has effective ways to protect itself in times of danger.

Collared Peccaries

Scientific name: Tayassu tajacu
Length from head to rear: 31-41 inches (79-104 cm)
Height at shoulder: 12-20 inches (30-50 cm)
Weight: 31-68 pounds (14-31 kg)

The collared peccary is fond of cactus.

How the collared peccary got its name is no mystery. It has a yellowish white band of hair around its neck.

Collared peccaries have the widest range of the three species of peccary. Their habitat extends from the lower United States through most of Central and South America. In this enormous territory, they prefer to live in the woods. But they also feel right at home in the arid bush lands such as those they inhabit in Bolivia and Argentina. Indeed, since they are often found as far north as Texas and Arizona, collared peccaries must be very adaptable. They are able to survive in a variety of landscapes, ranging from thick oak forests to cactus deserts.

Depending on what is available in their particular habitat, peccaries eat a great many foods. Like pigs, the peccary's vision is nothing exceptional, but its sense of smell is exceptional. Peccaries can sniff out roots and bulbs in the ground to depths of nearly 4 inches (10 cm). They dig out the delicacies with their snouts. They also eat fungi, nuts, and the fruit of the palm tree. In addition, collared peccaries living in South America eat bird and turtle eggs, insects, frogs, snakes, and any dead animals they come across. In Arizona and Texas, on the other hand, peccaries live almost exclusively on plants, especially cacti. They hold the prickly plants down with their front hooves and peel them to get to the juicy meat. The cactus plant is such an excellent source of water that the peccary can often go without other sources of water for two weeks at a time.

Without a warm undercoat, the animal has a difficult time when it is cold. Over the years, however, the peccary has learned some interesting means of dealing with low temperatures. For one thing, peccaries change their eating habits during the winter. In the summer, they look for food mostly in the early morning and again in late afternoon during times when it is cool. In the winter, however, they forage for food all day long, taking advantage of the sunlight and gathering as much food as they can. At night in their burrows, the peccaries lie close together, sharing their body heat. Collared peccaries have another mechanism for controlling body heat — coloring. During the winter, their bristles grow black tips. Because black is a color that absorbs warmth, this increases the peccary's body temperature. In summer, however, these black tips break off, and the peccary then wears a lighter coat to reflect the heat. In spite of these natural mechanisms for dealing with low temperatures, peccaries still suffer and sometimes die from lung infections caused by the cold.

Collared peccaries live in groups that sometimes number over twenty animals. They maintain a strict rank, and each peccary has particular rights and duties depending on its rank. The leader of the group is always the oldest female. She marches at the head of the line when the peccaries walk single file.

The highest ranked male is the "watchdog" of the group. He stands guard over the group and gives out a series of brief, loud cries if he detects danger. He is assisted in this task by the two youngest females as soon as they have lost their baby coats at the age of two months and have joined the ranking sequence in the group. Frequently, subgroups will also form within the larger group. Old and sick animals, for example, prefer to go their own way, but continue to maintain intermittent contact with the group.

The size of the group's territory depends upon how many animals are in the group and

Collared peccaries rub secretions from their scent glands on each other's faces. This creates their "group odor."

on the availability of food. A resting place is established in the middle of the territory. The boundaries of the resting area are marked by the males with secretions from their back glands. The peccaries also rub this secretion on each other's faces as a way of marking each individual and establishing a "group

Only two or three of the highest ranked females and the highest ranked male reproduce. Every six months, a female will give birth to two young — rarely more or less than this — in a hollow. Before the mother rejoins the group the day after the birth, she introduces her new babies to their six-month-old siblings and year-old sisters. Astonishingly, the sisters not only protect the little newborns, but they also help nurse them as well. Such generosity is virtually unknown elsewhere in the animal kingdom, and it is especially unusual to find animals that are themselves not yet full grown able to nurse their younger siblings.

In the wild, peccaries don't usually live more than about six years. Human beings are the peccary's worst enemy. Hunters kill them in great numbers for their hides. In

odor" that each animal will recognize. This odor is so strong that even humans can smell it and use it to identify the various groups. Peccaries that don't belong are driven away from the rest area when they are spotted. Land around the rest area, however, is not protected so fiercely. Different peccary groups share watering holes and wallow sites.

spite of this, the numbers of these adaptable animals have fortunately remained steady in the Americas.

Upper, left: Collared peccaries groom each other's coats.

Above: Young collared peccaries are reddish brown and don't change color until they are about two months old.

White-Lipped Peccaries

Scientific name: Tayassu pecari
Length from head to rear: 37-47 inches
  (94-120 cm)
Height at shoulder: 16-24 inches (40-60 cm)
Weight: 55-88 pounds (25-40 kg)

Above and right: White-lipped peccaries get their name from their white chin hairs.

Although somewhat larger in size, white-lipped peccaries are closely related to their collared cousins. The two species inhabit the same territory but the white-lipped peccary prefers to live only in the woods. They are only at home in dry regions in the southern areas of their territory.

The two types of peccaries also have similar diets. Like its cousin, the white-lipped peccary eats leaves, fruit, roots, grass, eggs, various small animals, and carrion. This similarity in their diets is unusual. Often, when closely-related animals live in the same area, they develop different eating habits so there is no competition for food. With the two peccaries, it seems there is enough food for everyone.

Most animals that live in the woods live alone or in small groups. White-lipped peccaries, however, form groups of between forty and three hundred animals. Their territory must be large in order to feed all of the group members.

Besides eating, white-lipped peccaries also love to wallow in the mud and take sun baths in wooded glades. Traveling between these activities in the dense woods, the animals

constantly rub each other's snouts and emit low, grumbling sounds to keep track of each other. The white-lipped peccaries have louder voices and a greater range of vocal sounds with which to communicate than their collared cousins. The light-colored fur on the chin and throat that gives the white-lipped peccary its name functions as a sort of light signal in the forest so the animals can see each other. They also find each other with the help of their noses, since their group odor is even stronger than that of the collared peccaries.

Chacoan Peccaries

Scientific name: Catagonus wagneri
Length from head to rear: 38-46 inches
(97-117 cm)
Height at shoulder: 20-27 inches (51-69 cm)
Weight: 66-95 pounds (30-43 kg)

The Chacoan peccary first came to the attention of the scientific world as two-million-year-old fossilized bones. For a long time, zoologists believed that this species of peccary had died out. In the early 1970s, however, Chacoan peccaries were found living in Paraguay. The Indian populations there had been aware of this peccary's existence for years. They called it the *tagua* and, unlike the Western researchers, they were always able to distinguish it from the other species of peccary.

The Chacoan peccary looks much like a collared peccary at first glance. However, a second glance reveals that the Chacoan is larger than the collared peccary and has a longer nose and larger ears. The Chacoan peccary also has longer legs than the collared peccary, which makes it a better runner. In addition, its collar is not as well-defined as that of its cousin.

The Gran Chaco, where the Chacoan peccary makes its home, is a large, flat area in the heart of South America located where Bolivia, Argentina, and Paraguay meet at their borders. It is very hot during the day and bitterly cold at night in this lowland area. While the eastern section of the Gran Chaco receives a great deal of rainfall, the thorny plain to the west is dry and dusty. But the adaptable Chacoan peccary is well equipped to live with these harsh conditions. For example, its nostrils are extremely large and act as a dust filter to prevent its nose from becoming clogged.

However, this is not to say that the Chacoan peccary has an easy time of it. It is hunted for its tasty meat. Its habitat is threatened by cattle that have grazed the plains since the 1970s. So far, the Chacoan peccary has not adapted well to sharing its turf with these new inhabitants, and the animals have

Above: The Chacoan peccary looks something like the collared peccary, but the Chacoan peccary is larger and has longer legs.

become increasingly rare. They may very well disappear before anyone has learned much about them.

Chacoan peccaries live in groups usually consisting of four, but sometimes up to ten, animals. Some members of this family also live on their own. Like other peccaries, they produce a group odor to mark both their territory and each other. In order to stay clear of the other two peccaries, Chacoan peccaries keep moving during the day. They follow paths throughout their territories, taking mud baths and dust baths, and are done eating by mid-morning. Primarily, they live on roots, acacia fruit, cacti and their blossoms, and other plants. At midday, they usually rest in the shade.

The Nearest Relatives: Hippos

A regular hippopotamus (*Hippopotamus amphibius*) can weigh in at approximately 4 tons, but a pygmy hippopotamus (*Choeropsis liberiensis*) is not much bigger than some pigs. Pigs, peccaries, and hippopotamuses all belong to the order known as Artiodactyla.

The impression that hippos are fat is misleading. Hippos are solidly built and almost hairless. The only noticeable hair they have is found on their heads and tails. What looks like fat on the animal is really thick skin. This skin can be as much as 2 inches (5 cm) thick. It functions as a type of wet suit to keep the hippo warm in cold water. The skin is also covered with a slippery, slimy substance that is white on the pygmy hippos and red on the large ones. This substance can be compared to the oil swimmers use for protection before taking a long swim.

Hippos don't actually swim, though. Rather, they walk along the bottom of the

vegetation. People also shoot these shy animals and catch them in traps. Fortunately, a good number of pygmy hippos have been born in captivity.

The larger hippos live in rivers and lakes and in the nearby steppes and savannas south of the Sahara Desert. Previously, they also lived on the Nile Delta, but they became extinct there long ago. They have also died out in South Africa.

These big hippos spend their days in the water or reclining on the shore. A given territory is usually occupied by a grown male that keeps a harem of several females. Sometimes these hippos form groups

river. They can be underwater for up to five minutes. When they poke their heads out of the water, it is easy to see how well adapted they are to their environment. Their protruding eyes and their closable ears and nostrils are raised just above the water level, and the rest of their bodies remain under water. This makes it possible for the hippo to see, hear, and smell what is going on in its environment while most of its body remains practically undetectable.

The pygmy hippo lives in the West African rain forests. It always stays near water, but it is far less dependent on water than its bigger cousin. The mother always gives birth to her young on land, and the youngsters learn to swim later. Pygmy hippos are loners that live on a diet of leaves, weeds, water plants, and fruit. Unfortunately, they are now threatened by people, who are draining many wetlands and cutting down the

consisting of one hundred or more animals. Other males are tolerated in the territory as long as they defer to the powerful, main male. But if a male from another territory intrudes, the two rivals will fight it out.

The hippos make their way onto land at night. With their wide mouths, they consume grass like huge lawn mowers and sometimes wander as far as 3 miles (5 km) from the water. But the water is most important to hippos. They even mate and give birth in the water. The female usually bears a single baby that comes into the world feet first. It takes its first breath of air before going under the water. It will nurse under the water as well.

Opposite page: In the evenings, hippos leave the water to graze on land.

Above, left: This hippo's yawnlike gesture is meant to threaten intruders with a show of its intimidating tusks.

Above, right: A young pygmy hippo from West Africa.

The Little "Pig" That Isn't One

Just look at these two little guinea pigs. But they are not really pigs — they are rodents. Guinea pigs belong to the family Caviidae, and they are probably the first rodents to have become domesticated. Their wild mice and rat relatives are smaller, more fragile, and wear solid gray coats.

Guinea pigs come in many colors and may have long, short, or even curly hair. They have round, plump bodies, no tails, and very short legs. Typically, these animals sleep all day and become active only at night.

The Incas, a nation of South American Indians, domesticated guinea pigs in Peru before the European peoples arrived.

Guinea pigs do well in captivity. They need little space, and they get along well with each other. The guinea pig breeds often. The female's gestation period is about nine weeks, and the litter size is rarely over three. Newborns develop quickly and can run soon after birth. A female is ready to mate when only one month old.

The three main types of guinea pig are the English — which is short-haired; the Abyssinian — which has a rough coat; and the Peruvian — which is long-haired.

Guinea pigs are playful and make wonderful pets. Like the Incas, people today have grown to love the little animals.

APPENDIX TO ANIMAL FAMILIES

PIGS
and Peccaries

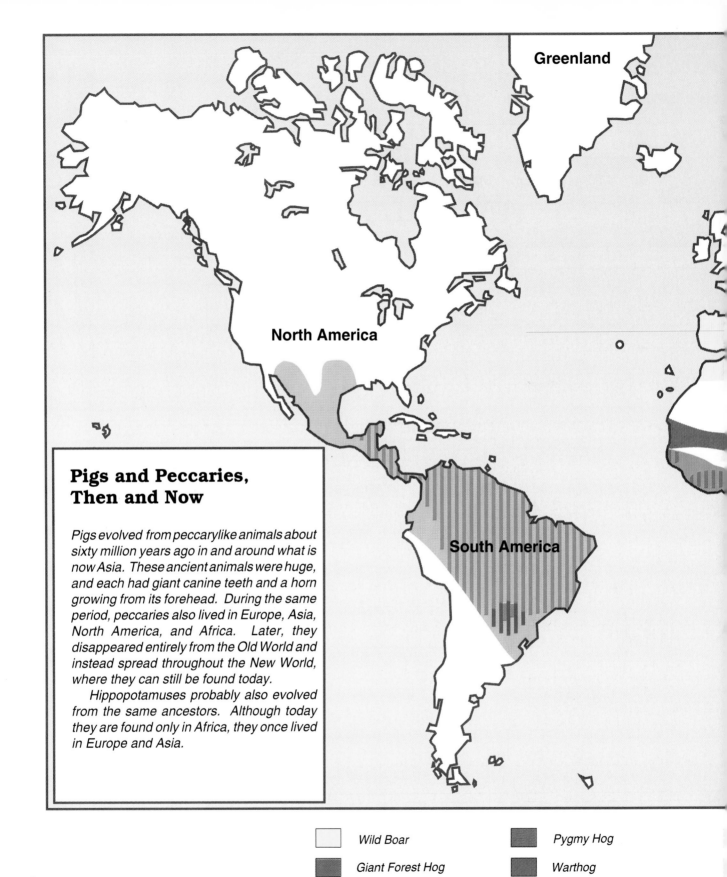

Greenland

North America

Pigs and Peccaries, Then and Now

Pigs evolved from peccarylike animals about sixty million years ago in and around what is now Asia. These ancient animals were huge, and each had giant canine teeth and a horn growing from its forehead. During the same period, peccaries also lived in Europe, Asia, North America, and Africa. Later, they disappeared entirely from the Old World and instead spread throughout the New World, where they can still be found today.

Hippopotamuses probably also evolved from the same ancestors. Although today they are found only in Africa, they once lived in Europe and Asia.

South America

Wild Boar	Pygmy Hog
Giant Forest Hog	Warthog

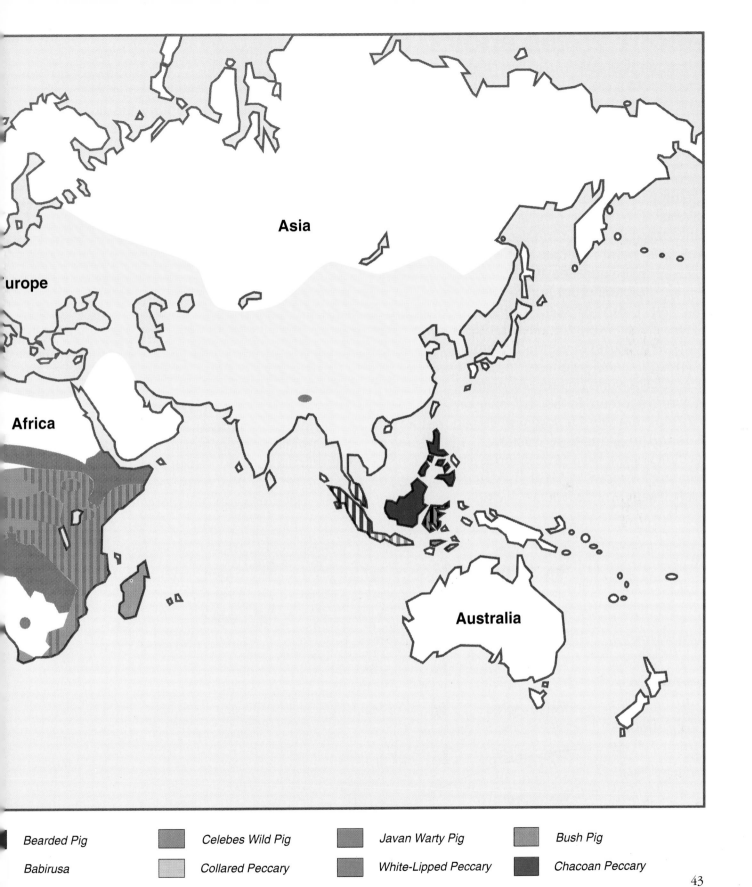

Asia

urope

Africa

Australia

Bearded Pig

Babirusa

Celebes Wild Pig

Collared Peccary

Javan Warty Pig

White-Lipped Peccary

Bush Pig

Chacoan Peccary

43

ABOUT THESE BOOKS

Although this series is called "Animal Families," these books aren't just about fathers, mothers, and young. They also discuss the scientific definition of *family,* which is a division of biological classification and includes many animals.

Biological classification is a method that scientists use to identify and organize living things. Using this system, scientists place animals and plants into larger groups that share similar characteristics. Characteristics are physical features, natural habits, ancestral backgrounds, or any other qualities that make one organism either like or different from another.

The method used today for biological classification was introduced in 1753 by a Swedish botanist-naturalist named Carolus Linnaeus. Although many scientists tried to find ways to classify the world's plants and animals, Linnaeus's system seemed to be the only useful choice. Charles Darwin, a famous British naturalist, referred to Linnaeus's system in his theory of evolution, which was published in his book *On the Origin of Species* in 1859. Linnaeus's system of classification, shown below, includes seven major

categories, or groups. These are: kingdom, phylum, class, order, family, genus, and species.

An easy way to remember the divisions and their order is to memorize this sentence: "Ken Put Cake On Frank's Good Shirt." The first letter of each word in this sentence gives you the first letter of a division. (The *K* in *Ken,* for example, stands for *kingdom.*) The order of the words in this sentence suggests the order of the divisions from largest to smallest. The kingdom is the largest of these divisions; the species is the smallest. The larger the division, the more types of animals or plants it contains. For example, the animal kingdom, called Animalia, contains everything from worms to whales. Smaller divisions, such as the family, have fewer members that share more characteristics. For example, members of the bear family, Ursidae, include the polar bear, the brown bear, and many others.

In the following chart, the lion species is followed through all seven categories. As the categories expand to include more and more members, remember that only a few examples are pictured here. Each division has many more members.

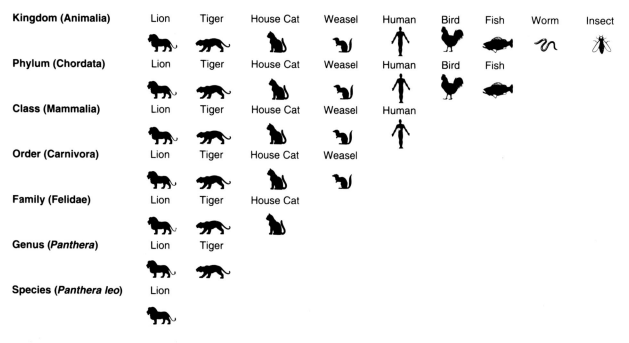

	Lion	Tiger	House Cat	Weasel	Human	Bird	Fish	Worm	Insect
Kingdom (Animalia)	Lion	Tiger	House Cat	Weasel	Human	Bird	Fish	Worm	Insect
Phylum (Chordata)	Lion	Tiger	House Cat	Weasel	Human	Bird	Fish		
Class (Mammalia)	Lion	Tiger	House Cat	Weasel	Human				
Order (Carnivora)	Lion	Tiger	House Cat	Weasel					
Family (Felidae)	Lion	Tiger	House Cat						
Genus (*Panthera*)	Lion	Tiger							
Species (*Panthera leo*)	Lion								

SCIENTIFIC NAMES OF THE ANIMALS IN THIS BOOK

Animals have different names in every language. For this reason, researchers the world over use the same scientific names, which usually stem from ancient Greek or Latin. Most animals are classified by two names. One is the genus name; the other is the name of the species to which they belong. Additional names indicate further subgroupings. Here is a list of the animals included in *Pigs and Peccaries.*

Wild Boar .... *Sus scrofa*	Warthog .... *Phacochoerus aethiopicus*
Pygmy Hog .... *Sus salvanius*	Babirusa .... *Babyrousa babyrussa*
Bearded Pig .... *Sus barbatus*	Collared Peccary .... *Tayassu tajacu*
Celebes Wild Pig .... *Sus celebensis*	White-Lipped Peccary .... *Tayassu pecari*
Javan Warty Pig .... *Sus verrucosus*	Chacoan Peccary .... *Catagonus wagneri*
Bush Pig .... *Potamochoerus porcus*	Hippopotamus .... *Hippopotamus amphibius*
Giant Forest Pig .... *Hylochoerus meinertzhageni*	Pygmy Hippopotamus .... *Choeropsis liberiensis*

GLOSSARY

adaptable
Capable of adjusting to a situation or environment. Pigs and peccaries live in a variety of environments – forests, bush lands, open plains, and even in semi-desert areas.

breed
To join (animals) together to produce offspring.

canines
The large teeth on a pig. In the babirusa, the upper canines of the males grow up and out through the upper snouts.

carrion
Dead or decaying flesh.

cartilaginous
Made of a tough white connective tissue called cartilage. The warthog gets its name from the six cartilaginous warts on its face.

class
The third of seven divisions in the biological classification system proposed by Swedish botanist-naturalist Carolus Linnaeus. The class is the main subdivision of the phylum. Pigs, peccaries, and hippopotamuses belong to the class Mammalia. Animals in this class, which inludes humans, share certain features: they have skin covered with hair, they give birth to live young, and they nourish the young with milk from mammary glands.

deforestation
The cutting down or clearing away of trees and forests.

endangered animals
Animals that have become rare and are threatened with extinction, usually because of human behavior or a change in environmental conditions.

extinction
The end or destruction of a specific type of living organism (plant or animal).

family
The fifth of seven divisions in the biological classification system proposed by Swedish botanist-naturalist Carolus Linnaeus. Pigs belong to the family Suidae. Peccaries belong to the family Tayassuidae. Hippopotamuses belong to the family Hippopotamidae.

genus (plural: **genera**)
The sixth division in the biological classification system proposed by Swedish botanist-naturalist Carolus Linnaeus. A genus is the main subdivision of a family

and includes one or more species.

gestation period
The number of days from actual conception to the birth of an animal. The length of time varies greatly for different types of animals.

habitat
The natural living area or environment in which an animal lives.

harem
A group of females that mate with only one male.

herd
A family group. Wild boars live in family groups in which there is a strictly enforced pecking order.

hide
The skin of an animal. The hippo's hide, which is often up to 2 inches (5 cm) thick, functions as a wet suit in cold water.

kingdom
The first of seven divisions in the biological classification system proposed by Swedish botanist-naturalist Carolus Linnaeus. Animals, including humans, belong to the kingdom Animalia. It is one of five kingdoms.

litter
The young produced at one birth by a mammal.

litter basin
A nest in which the mother pig (sow) will give birth to her babies. It is often made of sticks and leaves.

mammal
A warm-blooded animal that nurses its young with its own milk from the female.

migration
To move from one region and settle in another periodically, often seasonally. Bearded pigs undertake long journeys under the leadership of an old male.

omnivore
An animal that eats both animal and vegetable substances. Pigs are omnivores.

order
The fourth of seven divisions in the biological classification system proposed by the Swedish botanist-naturalist Carolus Linnaeus. The order is the main subdivision of the class and contains many different families. Pigs, peccaries, and hippopotamuses belong to the order Artiodactyla.

peccary
A piglike, hooved mammal.

phylum (plural: **phyla**)
The second of seven divisions in the biological classification system proposed by the Swedish botanist-naturalist Carolus Linnaeus. A phylum is one of the main divisions of a kingdom.

predator
An animal that lives by eating certain other animals.

species
The last of seven divisions in the biological classification system proposed by Swedish botanist-naturalist Carolus Linnaeus. The species is the main subdivision of the genus. It may include further subgroups of its own, called subspecies. At the level of species, members share many features and are capable of breeding with one another.

suborbital
Located below the eye. On an adult Celebes wild pig, the cheek warts grow so large they grow together with the suborbital warts.

territory
An area inhabited by individual animals, mating pairs, or groups of animals. These areas are often vigorously defended against intruders.

wallow
A pool of mud in which animals roll around.

MORE BOOKS ABOUT PIGS, PECCARIES, AND HIPPOS

Animal Families of the Wild. William Russell, ed. (Crown)
The Book of the Pig. Jack Anton Scott and Ozzie Sweet (GP Putnam & Sons)
Curly the Piglet. Cynthia Overbeck (Carolrhoda)
Farm Animals. Dorothy Hinshaw Patent (Holiday)
Hippopotamus. Winifred Rosen Casey (Golden Press)
Our Vanishing Farm Animals. Catherine Paladino (Joy Street)
Pigs Tame and Wild. Oliver L. Earle (William Morrow)
Spots, Feathers, and Curly Tails. Nancy Tafuri (Greenwillow)
Wild Boars. Darrel Nicholson (Carolrhoda)

PLACES TO WRITE

The following are some of the many organizations that exist to educate people about animals, promote the protection of animals, and encourage the conservation of their environments. Write to these organizations for more information about pigs, peccaries, hippopotamuses, other animals, or animal concerns of interest to you. When you write, include your name, address, and age, and state clearly what you want to know. Don't forget to enclose a stamped, self-addressed envelope for a reply.

African Wildlife Foundation
1717 Massachusetts Ave. NW
Washington, D.C. 20036

Canadian Wildlife Federation
2740 Queensview Drive
Ottawa, Ontario K2B 1A2

Greenpeace
1436 U Street, NW
Washington, D.C. 20009

The Nature Conservancy
1815 North Lynn Street
Arlington, VA 22209

The Wilderness Society
900 17th Street NW
Washington, D.C. 20006-2596

THINGS TO DO

These projects are designed to help you have fun with what you've learned about pigs. You can do the activities alone, in small groups, or as a class project.

1. Compare the features of pigs and hippos. What do they have in common? How are they different?

2. Pigs are a favorite animal among collectors. Go to a shopping mall or browse through a catalog and see how many different items you can find in the shape of a pig or with a pig on it.

3. Make your own "piggy bank" out of papier mâché and a balloon. Dip strips of 1 in. x 10 in. (2.54 cm x 25 cm) newspaper in a solution of water and flour. Carefully lay the wet strips on a 9 in. or 12 in. (23 cm or 30 cm) inflated balloon. When the balloon is completely covered, allow it to dry by placing it in an empty dish or margarine tub. When the strips have dried, carefully insert a pin through the paper to pop the balloon. Cut a small hole in the top of your "piggy bank." Paint a pig face on the balloon. Glue empty thread spools or corks on the bottom to help your bank stand.

INDEX